Love
Aisha
xx

Sacred Self-acceptance

A journey of healing through trauma.

Aisha Gordon-Hiles

Sacred Self-acceptance © 2021 Aisha Gordon-Hiles

ISBN: 9798775257798

First edition 2021

To you, and the little bit of her inside of you... Whoever you are, wherever you have been, you will always have you, and you are exactly who you are supposed to be.

Acknowledgment

I want to say thank you to every single person, spirit and soul I have crossed paths with since the day I was born. Clients, Family, Friends, Partners, Strangers, Teachers, and more. You have all helped and inspired me, more than you will ever know.

Preface

"All the events (in this book) that you hear, feel, and picture are real life events that happened to you, to him, to her, and to me. Sacred Self-acceptance has been of interest to me for most of my life. As humans, we go through so many traumatic trials and tribulations, questioning our faith, our purpose and our existence. That journey may not always feel beautiful, but it is beautiful to me.

As a counsellor, I help people process the footprints of pain on their mind, body, and soul, each and every day. Sacred self-acceptance is a reflection of just that.

Having not written poetry since I was in year one, this book challenged my own self-acceptance. You see, I am a therapist, yes. But first and foremost, I am human. So I am not immune to the pain that life throws at us all. I have to process my pain just as you do, and this allows me to help and understand you.

I wrote this book to illustrate the delicate journey of life that we will all go through, but also to give hope to those who feel constantly tripped up by potholes in the road.

You can do this... I am with you... "

S

The Apple tree signifies youth, happiness, and being healthy.

Straight out into the world, with no real
understanding.
Eyes too afraid to open, bright lights and
sounds expanding.
Where am I? Why am I here?
No answers she was given.
A tap across her back
Sent her body into rhythm.

Emotion rushed right through her, from her
head down to her feet.
Her airways opened and then came a sound
A sound she had no idea she could achieve.

This would be the first of many surprises she
would encounter.
It would be some time until she noticed there
was something special about her.

You see, she was born with something special,
a gift she had yet to find.
Her life on earth was sacred, protected by a
purple eye.
She was also born with something missing, a
part of her from another life.
A part she would never meet or truly know if
she needed to get by.

Who are you? Why are you here?
She asked as she was greeted with smiles.
Passed around from hand to hand
And named as somebody's child.

She had no choice in being here, or over where
she went.
She had to trust the ones that had her, that her
life on earth was meant.
For she was here for a reason.
One that would cause her great pain, joy, and
sorrow.
But for now, she must rest.
Close her eyes until tomorrow.

A

The Japanese Maple tree symbolises the serenity of
the worlds elements, peace and blessings

A gift from God, the universe makes no
mistakes.
Little did she know right then, she would have
everything it takes.
Life.
The thing she was given but never asked for.
The thing that one day she would ask what the
hell she was given it for.

A survivor, the only one out of two.
They say you are never really full when you
have lost a part of you.
A "good baby".
The night, she always slept right through.

3

"A happy baby".
Always smiling, and never blue.

Her smile, her eyes, her laughter, would one
day tell the truth
Of all the things she kept inside, the stories of
her youth.
For all that was in store for her would help her
understand
The pain that she would suffer, suffer at the
hands of man.

Inspired by everything she saw
She was fuelled by things around her.
So quick she learnt to take a trip
To places where words and steps could guide
her.

People would stare in disbelief, and doubt the
gifts that God gave her.
But she was young and fuelled by the sun, so
their comments never phased her.
Little did she know, these tools would help her
grow,
Into the woman she was destined to become.
And those people would call for her in times of
need, times when they were glum.

C

Creativity surrounded her, sparked her
interest every day.
She would be nurtured, encouraged, and
challenged, in a special kind of way.
A way that would help her grow.
And friends she would get to know.
In this place that would change her, where the
better and the worst would show.

Although she was inspired, she was frustrated
day by day.
And sometimes actions fired, with venom
instead of play.
She struggled to understand herself, and those
who helped her struggled too.
Her mother was called, again and again, to
change behaviour to new.

You see, there were things going on inside her,
things she could not explain.
She didn't have the words to describe that
thing she felt, pain.
Inflicted by her, him, and them.
Nothing seemed to make sense.
Although she was still happy, a part of her was
clearly tense.

Little did she know, he was tense too, that's
why each day he threw
Venom at her hair, her skin, and even her nose
too.
She brushed it off and said no words, with the
hope that support was due
From her friends or passers-by, surely the
teachers knew.

But no one came to save her, and so her
behaviour grew.
Pushed down inside, she started to hide, and
caused herself pain too.

But it wasn't all bad,
By the end, her spirit had grown.
But little did she know, she left with a gift, a
seed of self-hatred, sown.

R

Rage poured through her, and she struggled to
say why.
Countless times, days, and nights she was let
down by this guy.
He was supposed to be her protector, the one
to keep her safe.
Instead, he was the one who criticized her and
never kept to a time or date.

She didn't know it then, but there was a lot of
him inside her.
His mouth, his forehead, his banter.
Even his anger was alive in her.
Blissfully unaware until the day awareness
made it kinder.
She would battle with these feelings, a daily
constant reminder.

At night, she would stay up and cry
wondering why.
"What did I do wrong?" "Why did he not
want I?".
A pain she felt deep in her soul, that shame
had tried to hide.
If only they were together, her mother and the
guy
Then we could live happily ever after, him,
her, and I.

Her prayers were never answered. Her parents
did not unite.
Little did she know then, there was a reason
this end was not in sight.
A purpose for her pain.
Stable in her life he could not remain.
For he had to look inside himself and break
free from his childhood chains.

So, for now, she would pick herself up, and
take whatever he would give.
Carry on, day by day, feelings sensitive.
Every day, wondering why things could not be
the same
As friends at school with big families, cool.
Yearning, pain, and blame.

Envy. Contrasting to her excitement before
she met the new edition.
A pain so sharp that it threw her into
submission.
Causing so much confusion that she began to
lash out.
Leaving everyone to wonder why she would
scream and shout.

You never really know how you are going to
feel,
Until you are forced into the situation,
Feeling locked in by a seal.
She didn't have the language to express the
wound that had surfaced.

Or how it had left her questioning,
questioning her purpose.

Is there enough love for me?
Will she be the only one you now see?
Her mind, her body, her spirit was torn into
1... 2... and 3.
She tried to express her feelings, the only way
she could
Pen in hand, with no plan, over the girls
picture she stood.

The ink went flowing through her face.
But in that moment, she felt a trace
Of the excitement she used to feel,
And then shame started to reveal,
The regret she would struggle to heal.

If only she knew she had people she could talk
to,
People that would help her work these feelings
through.

D

The palm tree signifies bending but not breaking

Defence mechanisms would come flooding in,
When her ability to cope was wearing thin.
A conflicting feeling deep down to her core.
Her body would always keep the score.

Something told her she had to keep the peace.
So, she wrapped herself up, arms like a fleece.
Wiped all her tears and pushed back her hair.
She put on a smile like the pain was not there.

And in essence, it wasn't. It was confusing
you see.
How do you process something you do not
foresee?

Emotions, sensations, and a cognitive spree.
All bubbling inside her, under lock, without a
key.

So, until she would know, the process to grow,
To let go of the pain in her home,
She would carry her woes, defences in toe,
Like there was nothing to know.

You see, the body and mind are amazing
things.
They protect you more than your reckoning.
Do what they can to keep you safe.
From what life will throw at you with haste.

The juniper tree symbolises a journey that has taken many twists and turns.

So many things were set to happen, in the
next part of her life.
It would feel like everything was thrown at
her:
Pain, Love, Joy, and Strife.
And she would again begin to question why it
was her that was given this fight.

She found her group of people.
And met the second love in her life.
He would make her smile and keep her close
And then break her heart not once, but twice.

She would also lose her mother, on a twisted
and painful night

And there would be days when she would
wonder if she ever processed that fright.
For she was used to keeping things inside, and
rising to the challenge.
Taking what life threw at her without
knowing what she could manage.

She didn't know that this could destroy her.
Wounds seeping deep within.
Until the day she thought she would burst, if
she was pricked by another pin.

All that life had thrown at her, transformed
into anger and self-loathing.
She blamed herself for things she couldn't help
And sought solace from another him.

She was praised for her strength. Her energy
shining through her laughter.
But deep down inside, she knew that she cried,
At night for the things she was after.
You see the seeds had been sown and her
confidence thrown.
By self-hate, yearning, pain, and blame.
Constantly comparing herself to others, just
wanting to feel like she was the same.

The Lemon tree symbolises freshness, romance, and healing.

Enter a fresh start,
A decision she made that was backed by her
heart.
An overwhelming new adventure
Filled with freedom, excitement, and censure.

Her surroundings would shock her system,
And challenge her beyond belief.
In a flash she will have parted,
With the person she had started.
Taking with him a piece of her. Thief.

She would admire others from afar.
Deep longing and yearning in her heart.

With a false belief that from her, they would
want to part.

You see, she knew she was loved but
something was missing.
Causing her to hide behind a mask.
The thing she lacked most, she leaned on like a
post,
So, it was first in every room that she walked
in.

She used it to protect her from persons mean,
Who mocked the way she looked, behaved,
and everything in between.
She used it to pretend she didn't feel,
Attracted to those whom most saw the appeal.
Helping her to get through each day,
Hiding the hole, she was trying to heal.

Lessons learned, she would start again,
But this time older and wiser.
But nothing could prepare her
For the loneliness she encountered
Thinking it was the demise of her.

And once again her insecurities would make
choices,
But this time she was in danger.
And then she cried, in her room
Like a baby in a manger.

Little did she know, the trauma she faced was
sent to grow,
Her relationship lost so young.

To her rescue late at night,
In her honour, and filled with fright, he would
take that trip to save her.
Her knight in shining armour...
That day he became her father.

Her trust had grown and she was yet to know,
That love would become a barter.
The key it seemed, was in her dream,
And her vulnerability was the starter.

The Bamboo stands for freedom of spirit, regeneration renewal, and flexibility.

Freedom. A chance to explore her inner being.
She took her past and started seeing,
Inside her soul, and through stories told,
At last, her true self was revealing.

She took her time along this path,
Until she was too far from the start,
To turn around, run, and hide.
She knew inside her there was a guide.

For she had questions and answers too.
Little did she know then that "all that you
need is inside of you".
This journey would teach her and pull her
through,

Changing the version of herself to a new.

Easy it was not, that was true.
It takes guts to look inside of you.
To turn on the light and shine it right through.
No places to hide, no clue what to do.

She sought the help of others - few.
"It's not everyone you trust with what's inside
of you"
She held her head high and spoke words true.
"The shame you feel doesn't belong to you".

The Ash tree stands for sacrifice, sensitivity, and higher awareness.

A chunk of time forgotten without warning.
That's what happens when trauma has been calling.
She would look back with confusion, heart heavy.
Wondering "how comes I lost so much of me".

"But that's what you do when people need you" - Right?
You stay by their side and your insecurities deceive you,
Into thinking you need to come away from your lane,

To make sure that they can heal their pain.

But in reality, what happens is far from that.
Preventing their pain "you have no power for
that".
And the powerlessness will drive you crazy,
Whilst the exhaustion will make you lazy.

Things happened that year that were of
importance, you see.
Huge milestones in the journey of who she
was yet to be.
But as she looks back, she sees little evidence
of these,
"Life had prepared her to help those in need".

But now she wonders what that year could
have been,
As she realises "that was the year I left me".

The Cherry tree symbolises awakenings and rebirth

Crackle.
A fire had ignited within her.
For the first time she began to see herself
differently.
Attractive, womanly, sexually.
A new-found appreciation for her body.
A formation she had worked hard to achieve.

But just like clockwork,
She was going to get hurt.
As you do when good things are received.

But this time by people who had helped her,
you see.
Who had helped her in her times of need.

"I guess when someone no longer has use for
you,
Their true intentions for you can be freed".

Their actions would play with her fire.
Dampen the sparkle of its seed.
And she would not know where to turn or to
go,
In this world filled with selfishness and greed.

Thankfully she had others, and on their
shoulders, she could lean.
For she did not know where those feelings
would go,
If those others were nowhere to be seen.

And so she picked herself up,
And dusted off the sheen.
From the lies, so cold, leaving dents in her
mould.
Something she had learnt to do like a machine.

C

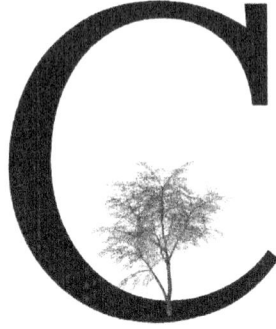

The Judas tree stands for the betrayal of the self

Constantly stepping on internal eggshells,
Brought about by her ever wondering
curiosity.
Is it your fault if you get hurt,
Because you couldn't let something that didn't
make sense be?

She had come so far and now was free,
To experiment with her identity.
She learnt different ways to express herself,
Using her clothes, her hair, and her sexuality.

Little did she know she had connected with
her creativity.
The thing that was to become the key,

That would set her soul free, and allow her to become,
The woman she was meant to be.

But for now, she was taking control of all that "is me".
Doing the best she could with her emotional debris.
But deep down inside, she continued to hide,
Her need to be accepted. Her heart's biggest plea.

Because in her mind, the truth would find,
A reason for them to leave.
Not trusting they could hold the truth she never told,
As her heart dangled loosely from her sleeve.

Truth be told, she thought if she got them involved, so deep - they would not try to leave,
Not trusting her gut in between.
Actions driven by the little girl inside her, that wanted to be seen.
That silently told her, speaking her truth would not make people keen.

Exceptionally testing, this year was to be.
Her confidence was blooming for everyone to
see.
She learnt to pose and look the part,
But that didn't change what laid at her heart.

New experiences would test her growth.
Take her back to self-loathing, feeling like an
oath.
Exploring the world with her friends, three.
Comparing herself, feeling increasingly
chubby.

She was let down by friends and family too,
And when life took her aunt, she transcended feelings to,
A place where it was safer, so she could get on and do
The things she needed to, to help others through.

And then she would experience a pain so new.
Shame and embarrassment would seep, right through
Her veins and when she challenged his view,
She would see how it is "when your family turns their back on you".

So, she turned to a space where no one knew.
A place where everyone thinks they know you.
Where you are so social, yet so recluse,
But there is always space to put your emotions to use.

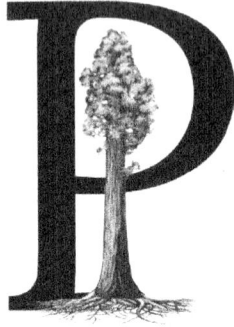

Patterns of her feet,
Scattered all around the world.
Each day finding more of herself.
The little traveller girl.

Twelve whole months of happiness,
For the most part at least.
That's when she wasn't dealing with,
The fears of his beast.

She had started to find her place again,
Growing herself around her pain.
Clawing back the little pieces of her sparkle.
The effect on her was simply remarkable.

Milestones obtained,
Her good fortune would stain,
And make this a time she would never forget.

And for once she could claim,
With no embarrassment or shame,
That she allowed herself to be happy, with no
regrets.

T

The Cedar tree symbolises strength, healing, cleansing and rituals of protection.

Time carried on.
Her good fortune stayed strong.
Bringing light to the good things in her life.
Like friendships, and family, and role models new,
And celebrations of years without strife.

She reunited with friends,
And with herself on the mend,
She took steps to look deeper within.
She followed her guide and tried not to hide,
For who she was, was not a sin.

See the little girl inside her had learnt a lesson.
"It was okay to show yourself through self-expression".
And with that came a great sense of security.
That she didn't need him to be happy.

She didn't have to deal with his beast.
Constantly dodging the wrath of his teeth.
One minute hot, and one minute cold.
So much drama she had never told.

And on the day she felt drawn to another soul,
She knew that his time had finally grown old.
And so, she broke the chains.
She cracked her mould.
Putting to bed the fairy tale, she had been sold.

The Willow tree symbolises fulfilling wishes of the heart, learning from the past, inner vision, and dreams.

A burning desire to give.
Share wisdom from all she had lived.
To heal others off the back of her pain.
To use all she had to make a change.

So many dreams she was able to achieve,
And real pain she was able to grieve,
And although life was far from perfect.
The key was gratitude, and it was worth it.

And when she was finally comfortable with
being alone,
Her confidence in her own company,
massively grown,

Out of nowhere as if it was magically sown,
A new him, would enter the throne.

And because things for her had been so well,
She gave her heart to what he had to sell.
Without much assessment or caution.
Thinking it was a continuation of her good
fortune.

And what a fortune it would be.
The gift she would gain, neither of them could
see.
But for now, she would have the courage to be,
Exactly, what she was made for - Glee.
Using her gifts intentionally.

N

The Hazel tree symbolises hidden wisdom, dousing, and divination, and cleansing healing powers.

Never again would she be the same,
But not for the reasons you might think.
For now was the time that when she wasn't
fine,
Purple would appear when she blinked.

Shivers down her spine,
Her energies becoming aligned,
She was starting to connect with the missing
link.
Guided inside, soul, spirit, and mind,
No choice but to listen and think.

Connections made and people to save,
She was finally getting the point.
Of all of the pain and torture.
Hidden memories living in her joints.

Her body would always remember,
The pain that she had been through.
But now she could see a reason,
Her mind changing to a new.

Reuniting with her God-given gifts,
Feeling the powers of God shining through.
The universe around her.
Letting go of what she thought he put her
through.

Creativity would save her,
From the year that would make her,
Consider pressing that button, rewind.
For she was sick of investing, and life
constantly testing,
The strength of her spirit and mind.

You would think for her sake, life would give
her a break.
But she knew that was not how it worked.
So trapped in her space, she continued to face,
And channel her anger and hurt.

Bring light to her darkness and shadows.
Toxic temptation waiting for her as she dozed.

Constantly pulling her to and fro.
Living life in an emotional limbo.

Creativity would pull her through.
In fact, it would challenge her too.
And life would strip her nude.
Of the protection that had carried her through.

But she knew what she faced was a testament
to,
The strength she had gained through times
old, and times new.
So this time, when her heart started to moan,
She realised; her new seeds had been sown.

The Bonsai tree symbolises meditation, peace, order of thoughts, balance and all that is good.

Excitement rose instead of fear,
As she bared her soul and shed a tear.
For the girl she once was, insecurities near.
All she had inside, now becoming clear.

Understanding the things that she had been through.
No longer would her mind be unequally skewed.
To negative perceptions, and things said, untrue.
"I will no longer be afraid to get to know you".

Connecting with her purple guides.

Embracing the tide with less inclination to hide.
Checking in with her body, to find out her truth.
Carrying with pride the pain from her youth.

Unlearning the things she learned to stay safe.
Not blaming herself for "the turn's life can take".
No longer yearning for things she was not yet to receive.
Accepting the heart she wore on her sleeve.

She would continue, on her journey,
Opportunities would find her.
Still driven by her insecurities,
But with a strong sense of self beside her.

She would accept the person she was meant to be.
And no longer force others to try and see,
Her worth.
No longer measured at sea.
Sacred. Self-acceptance. It was spiritual.
She was free.

Printed in Great Britain
by Amazon